KEITH CAMPBELL

SEPARATION for Elevation

Letting Go Chaos

Separation for Elevation
Letting Go Chaos

kcamproductions@yahoo.com

ISBN: 979-8-218-47405-8 (Paperback)
ISBN: 979-8-218-49207-6 (eBook)

Cover and interior design/formatting by Vickie Swisher, Studio 2020

First printing edition 2024

Separation (ˌse-pə-ˈrā-shən)

1) The act of separating, dividing, taking apart.

2) The condition of being apart, being separated.

Elevation (ˌe-lə-ˈvā-shən)

1) A raised place; high place

2) Height above the Earth's surface

3) Height above sea level

4) Elevating or being elevated.

TABLE OF CONTENTS

ACKNOWLEDGMENTS

First, I would have to acknowledge Jesus Christ, who is the Lord and Savior of my life. Without hearing his voice, I would have never separated myself from my natural habitat to allow him to elevate me in all areas of my life. To all the great leaders who have inspired me, the Rev. Dr. Martin Luther King Jr., Malcolm X, President Barack Obama, Pastor Noah Nicholson, Bishop T.D. Jakes, Pastor Jamal Bryant, etc., just to name a few, who endured a separation in their own lives and allowed themselves to be elevated and used for the goodness of mankind. Many thanks also to great leaders who were not mentioned because it takes a lot to separate yourself from your actions, thought and spirit, then be elevated to a level of greatness.

To my family, who has always inspired me, my brothers and sister who were there with me when we endured our own personal separation as a family: Much love. Much love to my mother, who stayed strong as she battled through a separation from my father, but allowed God to elevate her to a level of greatness as she pulled this family through.

Much love to my dad, for all your support over the years, and remember, during a separation, your mindset is what allows you to be elevated, be it negative or positive.

A special thanks to a few people I didn't mention but inspired me in a great way: the late Pastor Elston, the late Pastor Theodore Harrison, Fredia Williams (my second mom), Richard Elston Sr., Lamont Brown (the motivator), my grandmother, Dora Campbell, my late grandmother Johnnie Williams, Jerome Campbell, Juanita Edwards,

Stephen Robinson, Donny Jones, Carl McKnight, Jason Howard, Billy Jackson, Angela Cobb, Bonnie Webb, Jeffrey Smith, Pastor Joseph Harrison, Pastor Nathaniel Holmes, Angela Cross, Shannon Horton, Terry Anderson, Doy Harrison, Victoria Williams, Kathy Scarbrough and to all that I missed, don't take it personal, because it would take up the whole book if I thanked all who inspired me, but much love to all of you.

To my son Aaron Joseph Campbell, you truly are a blessing from God. As I endured my own personal separation, you at such a young age, allowed God to use you to inspire me not to give up. As you were going through a separation of your own when your mom and I parted, you put yourself last and allowed God to elevate you. The greatest thing that I experienced during my separation was God, but not him elevating me! Just to see how he took a child and elevated you during your separation to help me with my separation, I thank God that you're my son and now we can both achieve greatness because we have been elevated in all areas of our lives. Never forget what God has taught you!

To my loving daughters, LaKesha Campbell, Reagan Alexander, Taaylor Regan, and Taaryn Reagan. I love each of you and believe in you with all of my heart.

INTRODUCTION

In our lives, we tend to latch on to the very things that keep us from reaching our full potential. We stay in relationships that were over years ago or were over when they first started. We hang on to jobs for various reasons, such as stability, income (security), years passed, etc. But we are not really satisfied.

Some of us want even to let go of friends, associations, family members, etc., that we know are holding us back but, "I don't want to hurt their feelings" or "They need me" or "We're family."

But the truth is: this is the very separation I need for me to be elevated to a level of greatness.

The truth of the matter is that separation can be a very difficult process and usually we are forced, be it positive or negative, to make a separation from our comfort zone so that we may be elevated to greatness.

As we grow in life, we will continue to deal with separation as we elevated to different levels of greatness. I am reminded of a story that deals with a separation that we may all remember.

Without recalling the full story, our Lord and Savior Jesus Christ experienced a separation in his life. When Jesus came to the point in his life where he needed to be elevated, God separated him from the rest of us. Jesus spent forty days in the wilderness being tempted by everything known to humankind.

When he emerged from the wilderness, he was elevated to a level of greatness some can imagine but will never experience. There was also the separation that he dealt with when he died on the cross to be reunited back to his father in heaven. One day, we will all experience this separation.

The world was shocked as we watched Barack Obama become the first African-American president of the United States. As he achieved this level of greatness, he experienced some personal separations of his own. For example, separation from his former pastor, the Rev. Jeremiah Wright and other political people, to name a few. I'm sure he endured many more separation but these were some we all personally viewed.

FOOD FOR THOUGHT
Not everyone will be able to deal with your separation and elevation for greatness!

Many times in my life, I had to be separated from my comfort zone to be elevated into greatness. I recall when I was in eighth grade and I was on the basketball team, one of the starting players. My grades were ok, but not great but some of the teachers would pass us so we could play in the games.

When it came time for graduation and school officials were putting the list together, I knew my name wasn't going to be on it.

To my surprise, my name was on it, but how? Most of my assignments were not done and I had poor grades by this time. But I was about to experience a separation that would affect my life forever!

My mom came to me and said, "You are not ready to graduate."

My heart dropped because I knew all the kids would laugh at me for being held behind. After my mom sat down and explained it to me, I felt a little better but it didn't stop me from being upset or hurt. Well, the following year, I graduated and my grades were a lot better.

When I entered high school, I was ranked number one of all freshmen, with a 4.0 GPA. I also ranked number two of all sophomores with a 3.8 GPA. Needless to say, the separation from my peers allowed me to be elevated to a level of greatness. Not to forget the embarrassment and ridicule I endured for an entire year.

Now, I want you to sit back and enjoy this book. It will help you deal with your own separation and elevate into greatness.

The purpose of this book is not to offend, demean or hurt anyone mentioned within its pages. It is just a collection of my thoughts and experiences that inspired me. These experiences also helped me to elevate during a separation in my own life. So much love to anyone who played a role in my elevation during my separation.

ONE

THE MIDDLE CHILD

Growing up the middle child of four was not the best in the world, but neither was it the worst. Four kids! How could there be a middle child, some may ask but when you have three boys and one girl, there definitely is a middle child.

See, I wasn't the oldest boy, nor was I the youngest and I surely wasn't the only girl. So it always seemed as if I fell short on certain things. My older brother was looked up to because he was the oldest boy and of course, who could deny the baby child (my younger brother). And being the only girl has its perks. So where does that leave me?

Being separated from the very beginning of my life, I can't say that being the middle child and being separated didn't have its perks to me. When everyone else was getting their attention, I was able to get into myself and totally understand me.

I remember when I was getting ready to enter high school, my mom would not send me to a public high school. I guess you can say a parent knows what their child needs because none of the other kids went to a private school. To me, that was a great decision on my mom's part. I was in a school with no one I knew, so I had to fend for myself. This meant that if I was popular, it was up to me, if I was unpopular, it was on me. No big brother to follow in his footsteps

1

and no younger brother to shadow me, or no sister to call on if I got in trouble. Well, these became some of the best times I ever had, in high school.

My freshman year, I had teacher named Mr. Burton. I don't think I'll ever forget Mr. Burton. He was a well–dressed Afro–American man who took no nonsense. He always encouraged us to be the best we could be and get in touch with whatever personal gifts we had. I remember one year, Ebony magazine did a write–up about Mr. Burton for being an outstanding Afro–American teacher.

Mr. Burton encouraged me so much that I went on to become the number one freshman that year and the number two sophomore the following year. After my sophomore year at the private school, (Academy of St. James) the school closed. After all my elevating, I was being sent to the very place my mom didn't want me: a public school!

I attended South Shore Academy in my junior and senior years of high school. As things turned out, it wasn't as bad as my mom thought it would be or maybe I was better prepared than she thought I was. See, my separation in eighth grade– or failure as some may say because I was retained– and dealing with my separation as a middle child, prepared me so that I schooled myself.

I went to South Shore and hung with the popular kids. I never did anything spectacular but I didn't fall into the crowd and get lost. Being separated in eighth grade and going to a private school where not a lot of teens went helped me a lot. It helped me to realize that whether I was with the popular kids or not, whether I played sports or not, whether I had girls or not, I was still somebody to me and that's what counted the most.

For some reason, I'm compelled to tell this story about me and my brothers. Almost every kid has dreams of becoming a big star. Some want to be actors and some want to be singers. Well, my oldest brother and I wanted to be singers. Back then, the hottest group out there was New Edition. They were hot and their hit, "Candy Girl," was at the top of the charts.

Needless to say, my brothers and I formed a group and starting singing all of their songs. We even wrote some of our own songs. We did several talent shows and we were good. We won most of the talent shows we were in and the ones we didn't win were very close.

As we grew a little popular in the neighborhood, my older brother's ego grew, too. He wrote most of the songs, put together the dance steps and organized the harmony. It took a lot for the rest of us to put up with him but we enjoyed being in the group. Going out performing, girls screaming, winning a little money, man, we felt like New Edition at times. When we would finish a show and people would ask us to do another song, God, that was a great feeling, but all good things come to an end.

One day, we were in rehearsal and I had written a song. I sang it to the fellas and they loved it, but my brother blew a fuse! He said he was the leader and no one else could write or do anything but him. That was a blow for me because we were a group; not only that, he was my brother.

Well, after that, we never saw eye to eye again and the group broke up. My brother started doing his own thing with my younger brother in his shadow. Now I was getting ready to experience a separation once again.

When my brother and I separated, I started tumbling, playing basketball more and just grabbing hold of my gifts. It took this separation for me to be elevated in my thinking and confidence about myself. I took that separation, grabbed hold to my passions and realized that I would be successful with or without my brother.

This was not the only time I would encounter separation being the middle child. There are numerous occasions I can think of, but there are only a few I think need to be addressed that will explain how I dealt with separation as a middle child in order to elevate.

One situation that really sticks out to me is when my mom and dad separated. Well, all the kids went with my mom except me. I chose to stay with my dad and it was a heck of a price to pay.

I don't know why I did it, but something inside me told me that he needed me during these times. Needless to say, I was dumped on real bad by my siblings. They could not understand how I could stay with this man after all he had done. There were times I would go without speaking to my siblings for weeks and when I did, they would make horrible jokes about my dad and how I would grow up to be a loser like him.

I never viewed my parents as being losers, but as ordinary every day people who made decisions and all of their decisions weren't the best. Not only did I deal with ridicule from my siblings, but my mom's side of the family let me have it too. Uncles, aunties and cousins let me have it for choosing to stay with my dad over my mom. As a child and even as an adult, I never saw it as taking sides. I love my mom dearly, but I felt that my dad was really hurting and needed me by his side.

Sometimes I felt that if he did need me so much, he sure had a poor way of showing it. He would constantly be gone hanging out or working and I would be home by myself. This went on for a while and then I eventually went back to live with my mom. But I think those years that I lived with my dad, being separated from my other siblings, helped me to elevate in areas I would never imagine.

I was now able to love both my parents whether they were together or not and I was even able to deal with the verbal abuse my siblings gave me for coming back. I understood now that they were only doing these things because they were hurt and still, until this day, my siblings have not learned to love my dad, despite our past situations. I believe if my siblings had dealt with the separation I did, they would have elevated to a level of love that shows no boundaries.

That's not to say that my siblings don't know how to love, but it can be difficult to love someone who you think hurt you and you have not been elevated to that level of forgiveness or some may say, that level of love. In my case, it took me being separated from my siblings, dealing with the ridicule from everyone, being left alone by my dad and other situations to understand that you have to separate your own feelings from other people's actions and this will allow you to elevate yourself in love and respond to the person with the love they desire.

Separation does not always happen to the middle child. This can come even if you're the oldest child, youngest child, only boy or only girl, but it seems most common when you're the odd number.

There's a story in the Bible that talks about a great king named Joseph. Now Joseph was the youngest of all his brothers and his father loved him a lot. Some may say his father loved Joseph more than his brothers. Joseph was given lots of special privileges over his brothers and there grew a separation between him and his brothers. As the story is told, it grew great jealousy and envy, so much that Joseph's brothers wanted to kill him.

Well, the story goes on and Joseph's brothers did plot to kill him, but God's plan for Joseph was much larger than his brothers' plan. See, Joseph did not know that this separation had to occur for him to be elevated and fulfill his destiny that God had planned for him.

The Bible tells us that Joseph was not killed, but sold into slavery. While going through his separation, Joseph embraced his gifts from God and became a great king. He was eventually reunited with his siblings and he was very wealthy by this time, so he was able to support the entire family.

If Joseph had not gone through this separation, he would not have been able to love his brothers when he was reunited with them. Nor would he have truly embraced his gifts from God and become the great king he became.

One thing I do know is when dealing with separation amongst your own siblings, it can be a very trying experience but you must embrace the experience and make it as positive as you can. Try to remember that God will never put more on you than you can bear. When you come through this – and you will come through it – if you have embraced your gifts, you will be elevated to a level of love, spiritually, physically, mentally and morally that no one can ever bring you back from.

FOOD FOR THOUGHT

Once knowledge is given or obtained, it can only be taken if you give it away. No one can take it from you.

Name a situation where you felt separated or excluded and used it as a positive instead of a negative:

1) _____
_____
_____
_____
_____
_____

2) _____
_____
_____
_____
_____
_____

3) _____
_____
_____
_____
_____
_____

SEPARATION for Elevation

4)
_____

_____

_____

_____

_____

_____

5)
_____

_____

_____

_____

_____

_____

TWO

PRECIOUS MEMORIES

When my brothers, sister and I were growing up, we shared a lot of precious memories. Even during the time when we separated from one another, there were times when I would see my siblings and we would laugh about how much fun we had when we were a family.

One summer day, my brothers and I were playing softball in the park. My older brother decided he wanted to climb the fence. Just as he got to the top, his pants got stuck and he couldn't get down. I ran and got my mom from my grandmother's house, and then she went and got my uncle. My uncle climbed the fence and unfastened my brother's pants. My brother had to climb down in just in his underwear. He ran to the house and everybody in the park laughed out loud.

These are the memories I would hold on to when me and my siblings were separated. All the fun times helped me to realize how much I truly love them, no matter how much they talked about me for being with my dad. It also helped me to elevate myself to love people despite how they treat me.

One day, my older brother and I were playing baseball in the back yard while my parents were at work. Now, my parents were old school! Back then, that meant don't go outside when there are no parents at home. Well, we went outside. We couldn't find a baseball so we used our old Mr. Potato Head TM as a baseball.

I still don't know how it happened, but my brother hit that Mr. Potato Head TM so hard it broke the window. Man, we were in trouble, or so I thought. My older brother told me to let him handle it and I did. He left the glass there and took the Mr. Potato Head TM and hid it.

When my mom and dad got home, we acted like nothing was wrong. My dad saw the window and hit the roof. My older brother said we had been upstairs all day but we saw some kids in the alley throwing rocks.

My dad went up and down the block trying to find out who did it, but he never did. Well, Mom and Dad, if you're reading this book, you know who broke the back porch window now.

When I think about how much fun I had with my older brother and how much I've elevated in love, it makes it so much easier to deal with his ego now.

As I was growing up, I was the kid who would make up stories. I guess I did this to fit in or just make myself popular, but whatever the reason, I did it. There was one time when my younger brother and I were sharing a bed at my grandmother's house. All of the cousins were there and we had just watched the old "Creature Feature." Everybody went up to bed and was sound asleep.

Sometime during that night I woke up and had peed all over myself, including my younger brother. I knew how much my grandmother hated bed–wetters! I got up softly and changed my clothes and went back to bed.

When my other brother came jumping in our bed that next morning, waking us up, he yelled, "Somebody peed in the bed!" You would have thought it was a fire by how fast my grandmother got in there. She felt on both of our pants and of course mine were semi−dry, because I did lay back down in the bed.

My grandmother grabbed my younger brother and tore him up. He kept yelling, "I didn't do it!" and I wasn't about to be a stand−up guy, especially if you knew how my grandmother whooped butt! I stuck with the story for years that I didn't do it. So baby bro, if you're reading this book, I owe you one.

Having these memories in my mind and heart made being separated not so bad at times. When I would think about these times, it was like we were all standing there laughing together. My younger brother and I were always cooking up some wild games to play in the house, because were not allowed to go out when our parents were not at home.

This one particular day, we decided to play Spiderman in the house. The object of the game, of course, was to climb on everything like you were Spiderman and not touch the floor. We were having a blast until I stepped on my mother's marble table and went straight through it.

Man, I panicked and started yelling, "I'm running away!" My younger brother was like, "If you leave, I'm going with you," or I think maybe I asked him to go to with me. Anyway, we never ran away but we fixed it where we didn't get in trouble. We told my mom that we had the TV on the table and when we moved it, the table broke. My mother believed us and once again, our behinds were saved.

I believe when you're dealing with any type of separation, you grab hold to the positive experiences and try to recreate new experiences that will bring you that same joy. But you must not ignore the negative experiences either. You must embrace those also, so that when you're elevated, you won't allow yourself to recreate those situations either.

It's a horrible thing to be separated and then elevated, but go back into the same situation, doing the same thing again. I remember my dad used to say the definition of insanity is: "Doing the same thing over and over again but expecting different results." He used to also say: "It is a crazy man who keeps running his head against a brick wall and think the wall will break before his head."

Sometimes I wish he used some of his own advice. There was one time when my parents were going through problems and my dad had a female friend. If you don't know, kids don't always take the separation of their parents well. And we were still bitter at the way my dad separated from my mom.

On this day, my dad's friend had come to our house to take us all out. We all were in the house getting ready but I got finished first. I went out to sit on the porch and my dad's friend's car was parked in the front of the house. I went back in the house and asked her for her car keys. Stupidly, she gave them to me and I ran to the car.

I opened the door and started the car up. Just as sure as I started it up, I drove off. Keep in mind that I was only twelve years old. I don't know what was going through my mind or if anything was going through my mind. I drove down the street and turned the car right into a light pole.

My older brother ran down the street and drove the car back to the house. My dad was highly upset! I wonder was it because of the $1,200 worth of damage I did or because my mom would find out.

Either way, this would be another one of those memories that my siblings and I would laugh about while we were separated. And now, we are still laughing years later! But I don't think my dad finds it too funny.

Looking back at the time I spent with my siblings, some of the best ones were with my sister. Being a girl meant nothing because she could be as rough as her three brothers. If we had fights on the street, my sister wouldn't hesitate to help her brothers out. Not only if we fought on the streets, but she wasn't scared to take on her brothers, either.

One of the fondest memories that I have of my sister is when we were young boys. My mom and dad were going through problems once again. The money was short in the house and bills were piling up. The only thing to do was for someone to work an extra job. Being older in high school, that's just what my sister did.

She started working with my mom at Sears and started helping buy our school clothes. I've always said I was blessed to have a big sister like that. Sometimes I feel – or rather I know! – that I have the best sister in the whole, wide world. Remember, this is only my opinion.

I guess you could say that my sister dealt with a separation of her own during this time. She had to separate her average, teenaged girl thoughts and wanting to hang out with friends, to adult–like thoughts that must be focused on going to work and paying bills. This is a heck of a separation and elevation for anyone of such a young age.

Separating negative thoughts and positive thoughts can be a very trying task. In Psalms 51:5, it states, "Behold, I was brought forth in inequity, and in sin my mother conceived me." So it seems that our human nature sways more toward the negative than the positive. But biblically speaking, man was the only creature on the face of the Earth given the gift of choice.

This means that we can make a conscious decision to not harp on the negative thoughts and focus on the positive. The Bible also states, "Let this mind be in you which was also in Christ Jesus." Understand that once you are separated out of your comfort zone, then you have a chance to deal with God one on one. This gives God the opportunity to show you the error of your ways and elevate you in all areas of your life.

Trust me, once you have gone through this separation for elevation, you will be a completely reborn individual with a whole new perspective on life.

FOOD FOR THOUGHT

Separation does not always have to be physical. You can separate yourself mentally and be in a crowd full of people. Jesus tells us in the Bible, "Be in the world, but not of the world." To me, this means that physically you're here, but mentally, you're elevated to a whole different level.

What positive memories would you hold on to that could help you deal with a separation and elevate from it?

1) _____
_____
_____
_____
_____
_____

2) _____
_____
_____
_____
_____
_____

SEPARATION for Elevation

3) _____

_____

_____

_____

_____

_____

4) _____

_____

_____

_____

_____

5) _____

_____

_____

_____

_____

THREE

A BREAK IN THE CHAIN

In every family, there's always that one person that everyone turns to. Whether it's for money, advice, moral support, or anything, you turn to that person. In my family, that one person was my grandmother, or as we called her, Big Momma. No matter how we argued, whatever money problems, and any confusion, whatever! She was there.

Even when my mom and dad were going through all their problems, Big Momma was right there. You were not always going to like the advice she gave you, but it was going to the uncut truth. Big Momma could tell you about yourself and make you feel loved when she did it. She could say, "Now you know you ain't no good for laying around here with no job, but Big Momma loves you and she gonna help you get a job."

I mean, why would you get upset when someone was telling you the truth with love? The only time things become a problem is when we depend on that one person for our total existence; when you need them for everything and then some.

I believe that God does not want us to put anything or anyone before him. The Bible states that "Thou shall have no other God before me." It takes away from God when we put our everything into one person or object. This is when we need to make a conscious decision to separate from whatever it is and refocus on what's most important, which is, God first!

My grandmother was that one person that everyone dumped their kids off to her and went on about their own business. You know how back in the day, grandma raised the kids while the parents worked or ran the streets. When I was younger, I used to always see my auntie and uncle dump their kids off on my grandmother, then leave.

To me, this was a daily routine which became a dependency. They had become accustomed to knowing that my grandmother would always be there. My mother's younger brother was so accustomed to my grandmother being there and doing things for him that she was still cutting up his pancakes for him and he was in his mid–20s.

There's nothing wrong with a parent nurturing a child, but when they become adults, it's considered pacifying. We all know that a pacifier is something you give a baby to suck. When the baby gets to a certain age, we take it away from the baby, in fear that the baby may become dependent on it or it may damage their teeth. When we pacify adults, they tend to suck you dry and you become a crutch to them.

Somewhere in this cycle, there has to be some type of separation, so that the adult can eventually elevate in their own way. Sometimes in family structures, the separation occurs too soon! Our fathers leave before the young male is ready to be released into manhood. The mother befriends her daughter too soon and they become buddies. If a father leaves the home too soon and leaves a single mother to raise a male child, unless the child has a positive male figure in his life, he might be missing some important elements of his manhood. These elements will be missing because the separation occurred too soon.

Before the male was out of his adolescent stage in life, now he has to learn how to be a man from a woman who has never been a man. In most cases, the woman tends to pacify the male and he begins to suck her dry, possibly never leaving home or trying to get some other woman to take care of him and replace his mom.

Most men who have been pacified by their moms have never experienced the separation from being a boy to becoming a man. Don't get me wrong, I'm not blaming women, because you're only doing what is in your nature — that is, to be a nurturer. But as I said earlier, when he gets to a certain stage in his life, it's not nurturing anymore. It becomes pacifying.

The true blame should be left where it belongs: on the fathers. I can not tell anyone to stay in a bad relationship or subject themselves to unnecessary punishment by someone else. But fathers, if you must leave, try and take your sons with you or be a positive part of their lives.

This is what I call a break in the chain. It goes against the natural order that God set in place: for men to be the leaders and heads of their households. And this can never take place if the young male is never taught it. When my dad chose to leave, I thank God that we had uncles on both sides of our family that we could look to for positive support.

When it comes to my younger brother, I feel my mom pacified him too much. Almost every relationship he's in, he looks for the woman to take care of him. It took several years for my mother separate from him. Not to physically separate from him, but to cut off the pacifying. Of course, he wasn't pleased with the decision, but in the long run, maybe it made him a better man.

My older brother and I chose a different form of separation. We both joined the U.S. Marine Corps. Talk about becoming a man! If you didn't become a man serving in one of the toughest branches of the service in the world, I don't know what to tell you. I loved the experience and training I received in the Marines.

Sometimes when I feel like quitting, I can hear my drill instructor's voice in my ear yelling, "Marines don't quit, they work harder or destroy whatever's in their way!" This was the separation I needed, that firm foot in my back telling me never to give up. It helped me to elevate to a level inside myself where I will never quit!

Separation does not only happen for the male child, but it occurs in the female child also. We as parents must be very careful when dealing with our female children and separation. Like the male child, we can also let the female child separate too soon. Then there are times when we hold on too long and they become our buddies or friends.

I didn't use the word "pacify" because it is usually the mother that clings to the daughter, especially if the dad has abandoned them. They tend to use the daughter as a crutch, especially if the daughter is older. The mother tells the daughter what's going on in her relationship and in return, the daughter tells the mom about her own relationship.

Before you know it, there's no longer a mother/daughter relationship; they're buddies or friends. They're having drinks together. Mom has her boyfriend over and daughter has her boyfriend over. There is no more separation. They are now both adults sharing personal secrets about their lives.

If you are a mother, don't let this happen to you. When I was with my son's mother, this very thing happened. From the first time I met her, it was never a normal mother-daughter relationship. At six years old, her daughter would speak in grown–up conversations. I had never heard of such a thing. Like I said before, my parents were old school. When grown–ups spoke, you either remained quiet or left the room.

As the girl grew up and became a teenager, the relationship took a different turn. It was no longer, "Mother, can I do this?" It was now, "I'm gonna do this and I'll be back." By this time, the girl's mother and I had been together for a while and were living together.

For years, we battled back and forth about how extra grown her daughter was. This was such a problem because we had a son together and I did not want him to display this behavior. There were times when I would come home from work around 11 o'clock at night and her daughter would be laid up on the couch with some guy and her mother would be upstairs watching television.

Every time I spoke to her mother about it, she'd see it as no problem. I could never understand the logic behind this thinking. It was totally over my head. Things continued to get worse with the relationship. She was soon sharing things with her daughter about our relationship. In the end, we parted ways. As far as I know, her daughter eventually separated and went to college.

In every family, we must remember that separation is very important for our kids to elevate. The more we do as parents to hold on and don't let go, the more we hinder our children. And when they become adults, they will lack some of the necessary tools needed to become socially successful in today's world.

Big Momma's passing was the first separation in my life that was totally unexpected. Not only was it unexpected for me, but I'm sure it was unexpected for everyone else. There was no more dropping the kids off, no one to work out arguments, or anything else. Now everyone had to work out things on their own. It might have been hard in the beginning, but eventually everyone learned how to live on their own.

We all still have each other's backs but for the most part, we all stand on our own two feet. As hard as it may seem, death is a form of separation. A lot of times, it is the one that we don't want to accept, but it is a form of separation.

Even I didn't want to accept this as a form of separation, but I recently had to. In August of 2008, I dealt with another devastating separation in my life: my best friend, Pastor Schinova Elston died. This was a separation that I was not ready to deal with but God must have felt that I was prepared.

Pastor Elston was the one person who I could call on anytime. I could get in trouble and he would bail me out. There were times when he would just be there to encourage me. He was the one who encouraged me to start writing, doing inspirational music, acting and even go to ministerial school.

I served in the ministry with Pastor Elston for over six years. We were friends and he was my kids' godfather for over twelve years. So we were like joined at the hip. It was so tripped out that people starting saying, "Hey, that's Schinova's boy."

It felt good to have people refer to me in that way. We worked together on the same job for about four years. When my son's mother left me, it was a difficult time for me and my son. See, she did not only leave me but she moved in with a guy that was a mutual friend.

I was furious, hurt and confused all at the same time. There were times when she wouldn't even call her son. I believe she left out of our lives for about two years with no contact. During this time, Schinova was there every day and every minute.

22

At one point, he allowed my son and me to live with him because we had financial problems. There is so much more I could say about Schinova, because he was such an exceptional individual. Separation from Schinova has been very hard. I still find myself struggling with his separation on a daily basis.

But the big picture is: The separation from Schinova has helped me to elevate extremely in all areas of my life. Sometimes I feel that if it were not for God placing him in my life, I would have never excelled in some areas of my life as I have. Thank God for knowing what we need, when we need and how we need it.

FOOD FOR THOUGHT

Nothing is placed in our life to be permanent except God! Everything else is just temporary and will expire in time.

Name a time in your life when your chain was broken and you had to stand on your own:

1) _____
_____
_____
_____
_____
_____

2) _____
_____
_____
_____
_____
_____

3) _____
_____
_____
_____
_____
_____

4)

_____

_____

_____

_____

_____

_____

5)

_____

_____

_____

_____

_____

_____

FOUR

FAMILY STRUCTURE

Having a loving family can be a great experience! Someone to love you, support you, encourage you and just be there ninety percent of the time. Most people would love to experience this type of structure at least once in their lives. Some people have experienced this type of family structure in their lives. But someone or something altered the structure of this family. Usually when the family structure is altered, the separation between parents and children occurs too soon or occurs the wrong way.

A child can be separated from a parent too soon, before the knowledge and wisdom is deposited into them on how to raise their own children. In some cases, they haven't even been taught how to love their mates or how to support their own households.

Structure is defined in the dictionary as: "A union of parts" or the "manner in which a body is put together." We must understand that a family is a body composed of many parts. The mother, father, sisters and brothers make up the body. At any time, one of these parts can alter the structure of the entire family. The family could be altered in a positive or negative way. It all depends on what happens to alter the structure of the family.

My mom and dad were together for several years. When they separated, it was a negative experience for the entire family. I can't say what happened totally to bring about the separation but I know that my father had another daughter. This was a big addition to our family. Not only did this alter our family structure, but because my mom loved her family so much, she didn't separate right away. There were countless days our family had to deal with the thought of my dad having a child by another woman.

I know I said family addition, but sometimes it felt like much less. It felt like addition at first, but then it felt like division because now my dad was sharing his time between two families. Then came the fractions because we only saw him a fraction of the time. And in the end, it was subtraction because we eventually lost our entire family.

My mom fought long and hard for her family, but the child was not the only addition to our family. With the child also came the child's mother and a whole lot of drama. This woman taunted my mother for several days. Sometimes I don't know how my mom endured all the mess between my dad and this woman. Eventually, the mess took its toll when the woman started attacking my mother's children.

The woman made some harsh allegations about my older brother and other various things. If you are a parent, you can understand that this was the point in which my mother decided to separate. A person can do almost anything to you, but when they attack your child! They've crossed the line. This separation was way overdue.

In situations like this, a separation does not only help you but it can help others involved. The one thing we don't want to do is keep others from elevating because we are not ready to separate. This happens a lot in relationships. We hang on to bad relationships that are no good for us because of various reasons and we end up hurting others.

The separation would come quickly. One day, we were a family struggling to stay together. And the next day, we were separated. There was not so much elevation in the beginning of the separation. Actually, it would take years for us to elevate from this experience. My dad was the type of person who would never admit he was wrong, let alone take responsibility for his wrongdoing.

In order for you to elevate during a separation, you must remember that it's about you and no one else. What I mean is that you have to come face to face with your own faults. It is not a time to point the finger at anyone else but you! You have to take responsibility for whatever part you played. If you let people walk all over you, take responsibility for it! If you spend too much money, take responsibility for it! Whatever it is, own up to it!

This is the only way you will elevate because you are being honest with yourself. My son's mother and I separated and I blamed her for everything. I felt that she was the reason for my misery. In reality, it was my own fault. Nothing can become an addition to your family unless you allow it. We have the choice to separate ourselves from nonsense. We can separate from people who we know have bad habits or bad intentions.

See, I was in the streets at one point in my life, hustling and girl-chasing and everything else. Except doing drugs! I never separated myself from these things. Instead, I brought these things into my home. It added something to my family I didn't want and altered the structure. Once my son's mother and I separated, I was able to see the error of my ways. Now I was ready to be elevated in my life.

Many times, it's hard to elevate because we don't want to admit that we were wrong or have made errors. They may not be large errors, but we all have made errors. Holding on to an "I'm always right" attitude will never allow you

29

to elevate!

If my dad had taken the road of admitting his errors, things might have been different. Too many times, we went without because he took care of another home. When he left one time, we had no heat; then there was the time he took the stove and my sister had a new baby. This is why I say, "We linger too long in relationships that are not healthy for us and innocent people get hurt." It is my theory that if my mom had separated earlier, it would have given us a chance as children to deal with the separation and allowed us to elevate from it. Instead, we were never given the chance to deal with these emotions. So we dragged them on into our adult lives. We would eventually elevate from this but it would take us getting counseling of our own.

Family has been the center piece of the American Dream for centuries. The structure of the family is very important also. Let's take a close look at the father as the man of the house. Man, in the dictionary, is defined as, "An adult male person." Adult in the dictionary is defined as "grown-up; or a mature person." A man is also described in many cultures around the world as a leader or head of his household.

With most animals, the male is looked upon as being the most dominant or the leader. So in a family, we see a man as being, "a mature male person that is a leader." To lead means to guide by influence! Our influence, as the men of the family, must always be positive. It is very important that it is positive for the structure of the family.

When we as men choose to be negative instead of positive, we destroy the entire structure of the family. We must make a mature decision to separate ourselves from our childish behaviors. The Bible states in 1 Corinthians 13:11, "When I was a child, I spoke as a child, I thought as a child,

I understood as a child; but when I became a man, I put away childish things." Men, we must understand that as the leaders, we are the brain of the body. And medically, the body is not dead until the brain is dead. The heart can stop beating but it can be revived. Once the brain is gone, the party's over.

So men, let's put our heads on right and be the positive leaders we need to be because our families need us. One sure way is to separate ourselves from immature child-like decisions and elevate our thinking into mature adults. This does not apply to all males, but you know if it applies to you.

Now, let's turn our attention to the woman. A woman is defined in the dictionary as, "An adult female human being." Adult, we know, is a grown-up or mature person. It is also said in many cultures that a woman is a helpmate to her man or her husband. In some cases, she is known as his better half.

The Bible asks us in Proverbs 31:10, "Who can find a virtuous wife/woman? For her worth is far above rubies." The term "virtuous" is from a noun meaning strength, efficiency and ability. Here, it is referred to as strength of character as well as moral strength. As women, your characters and morals must be totally intact. You are the ones who nurture our children and they spend most of their adolescent lives learning from you. Our children start taking on their mother's characteristics even when they're in the womb. So this means as women, your character and morals must be intact even before the child enters the world.

Women, you must be strong because you are the glue that holds this structure together. You must be stronger than Elmer's Glue, nail glue and even crazy glue. It is very important that you have a high standard of morals and your character is becoming of a lady.

I have seen people put together model airplanes with cheap glue and they fall apart. As you stand strong in your morals and your character, those people whose morals or character are not right will separate from you, but those who are willing to elevate will stick around. A strong foundation sealed with the right plaster creates a sturdy structure. This then filters down to our children who must do their parts, which is a very easy one.

My theory is that children are to listen, learn and apply the knowledge given to them. That's why it's very important for us to teach our children that it is OK for you to separate yourselves in order to elevate yourselves. Our children must understand that to step out doesn't mean left out.

I teach my son daily that a man is not judged by how deep his pockets are but how much compassion he has for his fellow man. My daughter is taught she is beautiful daily and don't rely on your looks. Whatever we deposit in our children soon will come out. Almost everyone in this world who has achieved greatness has dealt with separation. If we get our children to understand that separating from situations that are not going to elevate them positively is OK, then we have built a family structure that will continue for generations.

FOOD FOR THOUGHT

One positive family structure can impact a nation of people.
If you don't believe me, take a look at the Obama family.
They have impacted the entire world.

*Has your family structure ever been altered in a positive
or negative way?*

1) _____

_____

_____

_____

_____

_____

2) _____

_____

_____

_____

_____

3) _____

_____

_____

_____

_____

SEPARATION for Elevation

4) _____

_____

_____

_____

_____

_____

5) _____

_____

_____

_____

_____

_____

THE BONDS WE FORM

While my mom and dad were going through their situation before they actually separated, my siblings and I would have to endure a lot of turmoil during these times. It would be very difficult for us. For a male child, constantly hearing your parents argue and having to watch your mom cry endless tears is a not a good feeling because you want to protect the woman who gave you life. I know there were times that I wanted to scoop my mom up and take her away to a place where she wouldn't have to hurt anymore.

During these times, my siblings and I would form a bond that was so tight nothing could break it. Each one of us would share a special experience with the other that would help us elevate from the situation we were in.

When I walked into the living room of our house one night, it was dark and all I could see was the silhouette of a person sitting on the floor. I could hear the sniffling of someone crying. The closer I got I realized it was my older brother sitting by himself. I sat down slowly next to him and asked, "What are you crying for?" After about twenty minutes, he replied, "I just wish God would take my life now."

I couldn't understand why a KID who was in his early teens would ask such a thing. But my brother could not understand how my dad took the side of this woman and her accusations against him, his oldest son. The words my father would use towards my brother would separate them for years to come.

There was nothing anyone could tell my brother at this point because of the pain he was experiencing inside. He and I would talk about this situation several times. I would always let him do the talking because I felt he just needed to vent about the situation. There were times I would make him laugh.

Hey, they say laughter is good for the soul. Through that entire situation, I believe a bond formed between my older brother and I that we would cherish forever. We form a tight bond with whatever helps us elevate from the separation when we separate from a situation. It can be a friend, sister, brother, mother, father or whatever. It could be church, a piano class, anything. Whatever it is, we tend to form a tight bond with it. You hold this bond dear to you because whatever it was that helped you allowed you to elevate from hurt and pain into happiness once again.

When we do finally elevate, we must be careful that we don't put our faith into anyone or anything that helped us elevate. We must remember that they or it is only temporary and soon will pass. Our faith must be in something that is greater and will last forever!

Being the only girl in the family for years must have been great for my sister, Daddy's little girl and all of those things. Yeah, I'm sure it was a blast. Until the day he got his own daughter.

Understand this: my sister was not my father's daughter. He met my mom when my sister was younger than ten years old. Yes, he was a great father and supporter to her. I'm sure he loved her like only a father could love a daughter, but when he had his own daughter, all of this would change!

By this time, my sister was a teenager and now my father had a little girl of his own. He would separate himself from my sister and devote all of his attention to his own little girl. Man, I'm not a little girl, but I know this had to be a hard separation for my sister. The only man she knew as a father has turned his attention to another girl.

My older brother and I could never take the place of a father in our sister's life. But we would assure my sister that she had men in her life who loved her unconditionally. We would try our best to be there for her, her three boys and her daughter, at all times. We would always look after each other's kids as if they were our own. The bond that we formed would help us all elevate from some of our past pain. We would have our problems, but for the most part, we would share love for one another.

It's funny how a child can be used to form a bond between adults or help you elevate from a situation. In the movie "Pursuit of Happyness," this man's son became his purpose for living and his desire to become successful in life. As I watched this movie, it really moved me. How does this man separate his own emotions from his situation and form a tight bond with his son? It was a bond that would not allow him to fall into self-pity but elevate into greatness.

The scene when the main character slept in a public restroom was a personal experience for me. I never slept in a public restroom, but when my son's mother and I separated, I slept on someone's basement floor with my son. She had taken everything with her when she left, even his clothes. She gave him one pair of uniform pants, two shirts and a school sweater, and one of the shirts was a girl's shirt. Laying on that basement floor every night, I would cry silently so my son would not hear me.

Many nights, he would call his mom and she wouldn't return his calls, so he would end up crying. At this point in my life, I had no choice but to separate myself from personal feelings about his mom. My concern was seeing my son happy and elevating from this situation.

There were nights I would lay downstairs and my best friend, Pastor Schinova Elston, would come talk to me. After all, it was his basement floor that we were sleeping on. He would always tell me, "It's not the dog in the fight, but the fight that's in the dog that makes him victorious, so fight until you win."

I would hold his words close to my heart and it would help me to elevate from that situation and many more. It would also help me to form a bond with my son that would inspire me to be great and strive for success continually.

When we bond to something, the bond could be so strong that it can pull us in the direction it is going or we could pull it in the direction we are going. That is why, during a separation, we must be certain that we are bonding with forces that will elevate us, not decelerate us.

I am grateful that during my separation, my son and I formed a bond with God that allowed us to love unconditionally. If I had never formed this bond, there would be no way I could allow myself to deal with my son's mom.

Don't get me wrong, it takes time to elevate from certain situations because we have bonded so tight to them and it has to be broken. We have to form new bonds that are stronger and more positive than the old ones. Then we must slowly pull ourselves away from those old bonds. The bonds we form sometimes can be so strong that they pull us down and we can't separate from them.

It is very important that if we feel ourselves being pulled out of our elements by something we bonded to that we break the bond. The sooner you separate yourself from it, the quicker you will be able to elevate from it. If you linger in it, the more time you will need to elevate from it. This is because you have allowed it to bond with you in such a way that it became a part of your daily routine.

I know of a young lady who was dealing with a man for several years. He had promised to marry her several times and had her sleeping in his mother's basement with her kids. Over the years, he never became a father to the children, nor did he come through with his promise of marrying her.

She had formed such a bond with this man that, despite all his lies, she was allowing him to take her out of her element. Whatever he did, she was willing to accept it because she was bonded to him, but he wasn't bonded to her. This is the worst type of bond: to be bonded to something or someone and they are not bonded to you. It may sound funny, but it's true!

We can bond ourselves to things that don't want to be bonded to us. This tends to happen most of the time in relationships. And it's exactly what happened to this young lady. When we're in situations like this, we usually get led out of our elements because whatever it is we've bonded to ourselves is in control. They can lead you anywhere they want you to go. Because they don't want to bond to you, it's usually a negative place.

This young lady was taken so far out of her element that she began to question her own ability to exist without this man. We should never form a bond so tight with anyone or anything that we feel we can't exist without it. The only thing we can't exist without is God. This is easier said than done because we care about our family, friends, etc. so much, but it is a reality. We should be able to exist if someone or something left our lives.

In the case of this young woman, it would take the man breaking the bond with her before she would actually move on. It took a while, but she finally got back to her element.

Forming a bond with someone or something is not bad. It can actually be good. The bonds that my siblings and I formed are actually good ones. We have bonded together so tight that we know when one of us is going through something without even seeing each other.

A bond is only negative when it drags you out of your element negatively and you feel that you can't separate from it or exist without it. Now you have put yourself in a position where there is no chance for you to elevate. Every bond that we form must either elevate us or we must elevate it. When we form bonds that don't elevate us or we don't elevate them, we become stuck at a dead end. The purpose of us separating from negative bonds and forming positive ones is to elevate into greatness. The bonds we form today will shape our tomorrows.

One type of bond in life that is very helpful is what I call a "50/50 bond." This is the type of bond where I'm bonded to you and you're bonded to me. We give each other what we need to elevate. The areas of elevation in life may be different but the common goal is to elevate. We assist one another with separating from things that have kept us from elevating and replace them with things that will bring about elevation.

Forming bonds like this can be a great experience because you give as much as you get and you get as much as you give. This keeps you from being bonded to someone or something that does not want to be bonded to you.

FOOD FOR THOUGHT

Be careful of the bonds you form because some bonds are not easily broken.

Have you ever formed a negative bond with something or someone and it was hard to break?

1) _____

_____

_____

_____

_____

_____

2) _____

_____

_____

_____

_____

3) _____

_____

_____

_____

_____

SEPARATION for Elevation

4) _____

_____

_____

_____

_____

_____

5) _____

_____

_____

_____

_____

_____

SIX

TOUGHER THAN LEATHER

When God brings us through something, he gives us the power to go through it again. Not that we want to go through it again, but if we had to, we could. Once you have been separated and elevated from certain situations, those situations no longer become a threat in your life. You now become a teacher and are able to assist someone else in elevating from that same situation.

Once my mom got over the hurt and pain of losing her family and allowed herself to be elevated, she was now able to help other couples that were experiencing the same things. My mom has been on her job for more than 25 years and now more than ever, her employees come to her for advice. To me, this is a great thing. Now she can give back all the advice and experience that helped her to elevate.

In helping others, we will have to revisit some areas of our lives that we may not want to. But it does not matter because we have been elevated from that. When we revisit those areas of our lives, we revisit them with a totally different attitude. Now we're able to look at the situation with our eyes wide open and not with our eyes wide shut. We see the situation for what it really is. There is no more fooling ourselves. It is what it is. This would also draw a lot of the game players away. They could not come with those phony games and think they were going to stick around.

Not even my dad was able to come around and play the role. My mom had stepped back into her element and was not taking any mess from anyone. I was happy to see my mom living again.

Sometimes we become so confident that we become arrogant. We must be careful to stay humble. We wouldn't want to hurt anyone like we were hut or accidentally misuse someone. To be honest, I've seen this happen on several occasions. As soon as we elevate, we get the big head or become cocky.

Always remember that your elevation from a particular situation is not only for you. It is also to assist someone else who is going through a similar situation. What if Barack Obama said, "I've made it now and I don't need to reach back and help anyone?" What if he totally forgot about the struggles he went through to get there? Then all of his struggles and efforts would be in vain.

A good friend of mine told me one day that struggle brings character, because you learn to humble yourself. I guess those who go through and don't humble themselves have not struggled enough.

When I think about my dad and his arrogant attitude, I say to myself, "How much more does he have to struggle?" I mean, he lost his family, his wife and everything and there's still no sign of humility. I guess it takes longer for some of us than others.

It would seem to be different when his own mom went through a separation from his dad. Talk about a tough woman. I remember when she told me the story of how my granddad left. She said she was living in the projects and he was on the police force when he left. I think she said she had about twenty five dollars in her pocket. She told me she could've gone across the street to the bar and had a drink.

Instead, she took that money and went to find a job. She landed a job at Marshall Field's and worked it until she retired. Not only did she work, but she raised her seven kids. I remember my grandmother would ride the train late at night to get home. My cousins would have to walk up there and meet her.

This woman separated herself from whatever pain she was feeling at the time, took her money and went to find a job. Not only did she elevate herself but she elevated her kids also. Almost every one of them went to college. This is truly what I call a separation for elevation experience.

While we are going through our own personal experience of separation, there is something inside of us that says we never want to experience this again, especially if it is a negative separation. I was once told by my mother that "if you go through something and it don't kill you, it only makes you stronger."

You can only become stronger by embracing the separation that you are experiencing. There is no way you can become stronger by denying that a separation is taking place or that a separation has to take place. To deny the fact that you are in a separation or that a separation has to take place only prolongs your elevation from your situation. Not only does it prolong your elevation, but you can not become stronger by being in denial.

In one situation, every day after work, this woman would have several drinks and then begin to swear at her husband. After that she would jump in her car and leave home for several hours. She would return home late and go straight to bed. This behavior went on for over a year. Her husband never addressed the behavior for whatever reason but I believe he was in a stage of denial. He was denying that there was a problem there.

One day he would be sitting for several hours waiting for his wife to return, but she never would. The next morning he would call his wife several times before he would journey to work. When he returned from work that evening, he would come home to an empty house. She had moved everything in the house out and started a new relationship.

When we choose to deny that separation is there or needs to take place, we fool no one but ourselves. See, this man was already separated from his wife even though they were in the same house. And he was bonded to someone who didn't want to be bonded to him. Understand this separation would occur by the person who was not in denial.

During his separation, the man would have to revisit a lot of experiences that he had gone through with his wife. These places had to be revisited so that he could come out of his state of denial. He would have to admit to himself that he and his wife were already mentally separated but in the same house and that a physical separation was needed because he was bonded to someone who did not want to be bonded to him.

Once these issues were addressed, he would be ready to be elevated to another level in his life. This would give him wisdom to acknowledge things for what they are and not deny that they exist. Our lives are full of things that we don't want to separate from, especially someone who we really love, or a person who has touched us in such a way that no else could.

My siblings and I would become stronger once we elevated from our situation. We all felt that we never wanted our kids to experience the things we did as children. No matter what, we would strive to always put food on the table, provide a secure place for our children to live and never put them in a position where they didn't feel wanted.

I've seen my sister work two full-time jobs just to put a roof over her children's heads. She would come home from one job and leave to go to another. There was such a determination in her not to allow her children to visit the same experiences she did as a child.

There is no guarantee that we won't encounter some of the same experiences but if you elevated from your separation of the experiences, then when you do encounter these experiences, you will separate immediately with no hesitation.

I strive hard to be the best father I can be every day, not only to my children, but to any child who is fatherless. I can't be every child's father, but I can show them a father's love for whatever time I can see them in life. Then it is evident that I have elevated from some of my past experiences.

During our separation, we must release all negativity. When our clothes get dirty, we put them in the washing machine. You add soap and the machine fills up with water. The clothes then begin to move around. This process is called washing. The dirt ends up being separated from your clothes. After that, the machine begins to drain all that dirty water out!

The next step is the machine fills up with clean water. Now we're in the process that they call rinsing. This process is to further get off any dirt that was left on the clothes. Once this is finished, your clothes are in the final process.

This process is called spinning. The clothes are turned around several times, squirted with water and then finally come to a stop. When you pull your clothes out, they're cleaner, tighter and they definitely look better.

Well, this is kind of like the process you go through during a separation. You are separated and isolated by yourself. You begin to get filled up with all the experiences you've been through. Now you must pour some understanding and wisdom into yourself, understanding that a separation had to occur and the wisdom to elevate from the separation.

Now you must allow all the denial, self-pity, guilt, blame and everything else to be washed off of you. The only way this can be done is through time! Just like a washing machine does with your clothes, the wash is the longest part of the process.

You must remember that without struggle, there can be no success. And your separation is your struggle. It is going to become your personal groundwork for success.

Now you're in the final process. You're spinning around trying to get back to your element, wiping off everything that has ever kept you from elevating in your life. Now you are back to your element, looking better, feeling better and tougher than ever. You might not be physically strong, but you are mentally tough as a bull. The only thing that can stop you is you!

Many of us will go through this process in life and we must remember that all stains don't come out in the washing machine. Sometimes we have to send them the cleaners for the stain to come out. These are times that we can't go through a separation by ourselves so we have to get some support. We might need the church, counseling or some other form of positive support. Whatever it is, we need it. As long as it is not negative, we should use it!

The most important thing is that we want to elevate from our separation and become tougher. I truly believe that if you go through a separation and you don't come out tougher, you have not elevated. We must become tougher and wiser so that if we are ever confronted with these experiences again, we will be able to stand against them.

FOOD FOR THOUGHT

Every experience you go through will soon prove how tough you really are.

Think about a situation that you went through that made you tougher:

1) _____
_____
_____
_____
_____
_____

2) _____
_____
_____
_____
_____
_____

3) _____
_____
_____
_____
_____
_____

SEPARATION for Elevation

4) _____
_____
_____
_____
_____
_____

5) _____
_____
_____
_____
_____
_____

SEVEN

WHAT'S MY ROLE?

Usually after a separation, whether it was positive or negative, we tend to find ourselves in an identity crisis. This does not always happen in a positive separation because in this kind of separation we have usually given as much as we've taken. When we endure a positive separation, there is usually some connection still there because we have allowed ourselves to be elevated or to elevate whatever it was we were separated from.

If you separate from a relationship positively, there is usually a connection there with the other person, but not because you still love them or want to be with them. Usually it's because in some way you both were a positive influence on each other. In other words, you've helped one another elevate in some way.

During a negative separation, we tend to struggle with our identity. If you say this is not true, think again! When we are separated from something negatively, ninety percent of the time, it means we stayed too long. This means somehow you were taken out of your element and if you're not in your element, you don't know who you are at the time. So now you are dealing with an identity crisis or trying to find out what's your role in life.

It's ok because at one time or another, we all deal with the tough decision of finding out what our role is. My dad and mom separated when my siblings and I were all teenagers or younger. The entire family would struggle for years to find out what their roles were in life or how to get back to their element. As we struggled to find our roles, we would share our own personal experiences.

As I struggled to find my role, I would find myself consistently searching for the stability and structure I was missing from my family. There were numerous times that I would get involved with women and attach myself to their families in search of what I missing.

It would also be the time when I sold drugs as a way of being accepted. When I sold drugs I was at the top of my game. I had girls, money, people who I thought were friends, clothes and more. All these things gave me a false sense of acceptance. I would deal with some horrible relationships before I would actually realize that what I was searching for could not be found in anyone else but me.

People would use me because they knew I was not secure in who I was. When we are out of our role or element, other individuals usually can pick up on this. There is usually some sign that we give that allows people to know that we are pretending or putting up a fraud.

Sometimes, we can put up such a good fraud that we fool ourselves. There would be times that I was selling drugs and I would have to do things that were totally out of my element. Then later that evening or the next day, I would think about what I had done.

One sure way that you know that you're operating out of your element or that you don't know what your role is: you will have no peace of mind. When we know who we are and have established our destiny or purpose, we have inner peace. If you take a football player and put him on the basketball court, nine times out of ten, he will fail. Not saying that he won't do well or score points, but he will not perform to the fullest of his potential.

My oldest brother was always the type that was good with his hands. I mean, he was a hard worker and could fix cars well. The only problem my oldest brother experienced was his ego. He had an ego that was larger than life. It was like no one else could do anything great but him. I mean, if you didn't think he was the top dog, he didn't want to deal with you.

The majority of this ego came from the separation with my dad and the way the separation took place. He wanted to be the father figure and protector to everyone but that can't happen if you don't know your role. My brother was torn between being a kid and trying to be a man, not to count all the anger he had inside. This inner battle would go on for years, with him trying to suppress an ego that was built on top of anger and disappointment.

This would put my brother in a position where he would struggle with several relationships for years. It would also cause he and I to lose touch several times, especially the one time when he came to my house and threatened to fight me in front of my kids. It would be a long time before we would speak after that incident. Understand that at this time in his life, he had not discovered his role. He was still operating out of his element.

My parents had always taught us to be loving and supportive of one another, so my brother was operating out of his element. He was still struggling with being the father figure to everyone. It may seem strange, but as an adult, he still struggled with this. If we never confront our issues, we will never separate from them and find our roles in life.

It would take my brother going to church and becoming a minister before he would confront these issues. After he confronted these issues, he would separate himself from them and elevate in love. Today my brother is a powerful man of God and has a loving family. He traded in his ego for a spirit of humility. It is a blessing to see him operating in his element and understanding his role in life.

We all have a role in life and knowing who we are helps us to operate in that role. Separating from anyone or anything in life that keeps you from knowing who you are is a giant step in the right direction. It took me being separated by myself for more than two years to actually understand my role in life and operate in my element once again. I had to confront the divorce of my parents, losing my son's mother and other personal issues before I could separate from them.

It would take me understanding and forgiving myself and others for whatever happened. This would come through a lot of talking, prayer, crying and accepting my part in whatever took place. Once that was over, I could process the hurt, disappointment and self-pity. Now I was able to operate in my element of love once again. I also knew my role in life. It feels real good once you elevate from an identity crisis to actually knowing who you are. This makes you feel like you can conquer the world.

I don't know about conquering the world, but you sure can change it. When we know our role in life and operate in our elements, we control our destiny. When I think about how my mom separated from my dad and how she struggled with finding her role, it brings a smile to my face. Not in how she struggled, but how she came out on top.

The times my mom would sit up crying at night wondering if there were something wrong with her, not understanding how her husband left his family and had another child, were some serious issues that could cause anyone to

lose focus of who they are. As my mom confronted these issues over the years, it is amazing to see the woman of God
that she has become now. She can stand in my dad's face
and hold a conversation without coming out of her element
or losing focus on who she is. The very thought of seeing
her being elevated to this level brings joy to my heart.

Knowing our role in life starts when we are young. We
search long and hard to find that one place where we are
accepted and needed. And once we find it, we are usually
at peace inside ourselves. It is when we allow something or
someone to make us forget our role that we become lost.

Imagine a child getting lost from their parents in a de-
partment store. They begin to panic, they cry, scream and
run around looking for the parents. Well, this is what it's
like when we're not operating in our element or don't know
our role in life. We all have different elements which make
us who we are but our elements help us to define our role
in life.

Let's just say you're an honest and talkative person.
Those are the elements that, nine times out of ten, will define your role in life. You may be a preacher, teacher or
something that deals with talking and being honest. We
must understand that before we can help anyone else, we
must first understand who we are and our role in life. How
can you teach someone their ABC's and you don't know
your ABC's?

If I had not elevated from my separation and learned
my role in life, I would not be able to assist my stepson
with finding his role in life. He is someone who wants to be
a cool, tough guy. I truly understand the need to be accepted by your peers but we must do this by being ourselves.
As I said, when we pretend that we're something that we're
not or act outside our elements to be accepted, somehow,
someone in the crowd will expose us for who we really are.

When we realize our role in life and operate in our elements, we not only affect our lives but we usually affect the lives of those around us. This can become a domino effect and not only affect people around us but people who are not in our circle.

Many people live their entire lives without understanding their role and operating outside their elements. Once you realize your role in life and operate in your elements, every day will be a day of progress and teaching. You will learn more about your role and elements daily. Then you will deposit these gifts into others.

If a man realizes his role and operates in his elements, he will then deposit this in his son and they will deposit it in their sons. The same thing applies for women. If they operate in their elements and realize their roles, they will deposit this in their daughters and their daughters will deposit it in their daughters.

After my siblings and I realized our roles, we were able to be better parents to our kids and deposit our gifts into them. After all we had been through and come out of, it felt real good to deposit this knowledge in someone else. After you have experienced a separation and elevated from it, and truly realized your role, but also operate in your elements, you will find excitement in sharing your knowledge and gifts with the world.

FOOD FOR THOUGHT

Without an understanding of who you are, you'll never understand what to do or how to do it.

When was there a time in your life that you didn't know your role?

1) _____
_____
_____
_____
_____
_____

2) _____
_____
_____
_____
_____

3) _____
_____
_____
_____
_____

SEPARATION for Elevation

4)

_____

_____

_____

_____

_____

_____

5)

_____

_____

_____

_____

_____

_____

EIGHT

DÉJÀ VU

Déjà vu is a feeling of having been in a place or experienced something before. Everyone has already experienced this or will experience this at least once in their lifetime. When we go through a separation and elevate from it, this does not make us invincible. We can still be confronted with some of the same situations we just elevated from. What makes the difference is how we react to the situation this time around.

The majority of the time, if we've allowed ourselves to elevate the first time around, during the second time, we won't allow ourselves to even go part of the way through the situation. For some reason, I don't think my younger brother ever totally elevated from our past experiences with our parents. It just seemed that if he had elevated, he would have stopped a lot of situation in their tracks— some of the same situations we faced as kids and you can't recognize them! You can never elevate to the next level until you pass the one that you're on. How many times must we take the same test before we pass it?

Several times, I would be confronted with some of the bad relationship problems that I experienced with my son's mother. This one particular relationship that I was in had déjà vu all over it, from the way I met the woman to the way we talked on the phone. I could see myself headed down the same path once again. Before I knew it, I had erased the woman's number out of my phone. Now this woman might have been different, but I didn't want to take a chance.

When we have been elevated, we must always watch for the warning signs, not only in relationships but in life. There was the one time where I was living with just my son and he did something that I thought was really wrong. I was very angry and was ready to start using profanity at him. Right then, I noticed the warning signs and I remembered how my dad used to talk down to us. So I backed up, prayed and approached my son with love.

The very thought of reliving those verbally abusive days and have my son have to live through what I overcame made me think. That's why it is so important for us to elevate when we go through a separation of any kind. If we don't, then when we are faced with déjà vu experiences, we will relive the whole experience again.

It would take me a while before I totally elevated from this on particular situation. I would be confronted with it over and over again before I realized that it was déjà vu. I thought it was different because I was experiencing it with different people.

In almost every relationship I got in, I went out of my way to be whatever the person wanted me to be. This not only happened with relationships I was in, but even with my friends. My other friends would call me on it and tell me to just be myself. Many times, a déjà vu experience does not happen with the same person, nor does it occur in the same place. It is we that are experiencing the same situation once again.

A lot of us will not elevate from certain situations because we fool ourselves and say that it is not the same thing because a different person is involved or it happens in a different place. The reality of it is that it's the same thing going on and until you elevate from it, you will continue to have a déjà vu experience.

Since my dad left my mom, he has experienced the same thing with other women. Somewhere in his experiences, he must understand that no elevation has taken place from his separation.

When I first became employed with the school system, I treated it just like I did jobs in the past. There was no commitment! The only thing that was on my mind was getting a paycheck. This behavior only got me what I had gotten from other jobs: a boss continually down my throat, a bad reputation and no advancement. It was a déjà vu experience happening.

Before I knew it, I stepped back and realized what I was doing. I was setting myself up to get the same results that I had in the past. Now if I didn't want to relive these experiences again, I would have to prove to myself that I had elevated from my past experiences. Well, I did!

It would take a while for people to put my past behind me and a lot of work on my part to forget the old me. After a year or two, I had proven that I had changed. I got a promotion to Dean's Assistant. I've earned the respect of my supervisors as being totally organized. They can come to me for anything and I will have it ASAP. This was one déjà vu experience that I was not going to relive.

Believe it or not, but our déjà vu experiences tell us a lot about ourselves. It helps us to understand how much we have really elevated from past experiences in our lives or it can tell us if we've elevated at all. If we relive an entire negative experience again, then we have not elevated from that experience. That's not saying that we won't revisit a negative experience to help someone else elevate from the same thing.

It is when we are confronted with a negative déjà vu experience and relive the entire experience that we find ourselves not being elevated at all. Our attitude toward negative déjà vu experiences must be, "I refuse to relive this chapter in my life all over again."

Remember, we are not talking about death because this is the one thing that none of us can control. This is pertaining to other negative things in our lives that we have control over. Many of us don't want to relive negative experiences, especially ones that we've overcome.

There are three things that I use that keep from reliving a negative déjà vu experience. First, I always recognize the warning sign. If it walks like a duck and quacks like a duck, then it is a duck. Second, I bring myself to remember the pain I went through and how hard it was to elevate from that experience. Pain has a way of making us not want to go through a negative experience again. Third, I separate from it. If I see a speeding car coming and don't move, then I want to be hit.

Now, these may not work for you, but I have found them to be very helpful in my life. They have kept me from reliving some horrible experiences in my life. One thing for sure is we all must develop a plan on how to deal with a negative déjà vu experience.

A young lady who was very close to me continues to experience déjà vu, but does not realize she is experiencing it. Every school that she goes to, she ends up in a fight with other girls. The thing is that all or most of the altercations were caused by her. Of course, she would never take the blame, but it is the same story in every school. I would say that it is truly a negative déjà vu experience: every place you go, people want to fight you because of your mouth.

This young lady has to really sit down and assess the situations. She must ask herself, "Does everyone not like me, am I really that bad, or is it something that I'm doing to draw this attention to myself?" After recognizing the problem, she has to ask herself, "Do I really want this behavior to continue?" If she does not, then it is time to make a change.

She should try making some new friends and see if she ends up in the same situation. If not, then she's changed for the better. If so, then she needs to further separate herself from her old behavior and elevate to higher ground. This can be done by getting around some positive influences or developing a plan for when these negative experiences occur.

For many of us, the ones who we are around can help us to recognize warning signs, so we won't have to relive a negative déjà vu experience. Many times, my friend Pastor Schinova Elston would see me headed into a negative déjà vu experience and he would stop me or at least warn me. It may seem strange, but those who are close to us can tell when we are headed down that same negative path again. And it is a true friend who will warn you before you take that fall.

This does not mean that they will know every negative experience that you've been through. But they can warn you about the ones they know about. More than anything, though, it is our responsibility to know ourselves. If you know yourself, then you can prevent a lot of negative experiences from happening twice.

FOOD FOR THOUGHT

If we see the warning signs and don't take another path or stop, then we want to be on the negative path!

When have you encountered a negative déjà vu experience and stopped it in its tracks?

1) _____

_____

_____

_____

_____

_____

2) _____

_____

_____

_____

_____

3) _____

_____

_____

_____

_____

4)

_____

_____

_____

_____

_____

5)

_____

_____

_____

_____

_____

NINE

BEFORE I LET GO

Letting go! This can be a very difficult process or a very difficult decision for us to make. When we think of letting go, we think of losing something or someone forever. The reality of it is that sometimes we let go just to get back to ourselves. We have held on so much that we have become comfortable, dependent or just plain content with our situation. One of the biggest parts of letting go is to realize that you can exist without this object in your life. Maybe it can be just putting that object in its proper perspective.

In other words, seeing it for what it really is can be a great way of start your letting go process. How many times have you stepped back and accepted people or situations for what they were and it made you feel better? This does not mean take the back seat to things that totally need to change. That's why we have had our great leaders of the past.

I'm talking about letting go of nonsense that is taking us nowhere. There is an old saying that goes, "Nothing from nothing leaves nothing." My grandmother used to always tell us that if a man is drowning and you jump in the water after him, but you can't swim, then you both drown. My dad would say, "You can lead a horse to water but you can't make him drink."

After you've done your best, it is my theory that you must let it go. When we hold on too long, we end up ruining ourselves or we ruin someone else. If you give a man a fish, you feed him for a day, but if you teach him to fish, he'll feed himself for a lifetime.

I know some people want to argue with this, but there even comes a time when we have to let our kids go. There are many times when I've seen parents hold on to kids and they ruin their lives. These kids become so dependent on their parents that they go through life looking for someone else to treat them like their parents did.

Now, it doesn't mean if you have a virtuous woman for a mom or a stand-up man for a father that you shouldn't look for someone with these qualities. But to have someone pamper you like your parents did is ridiculous. When we hold on to our kids like that, we never offer them the chance to separate and elevate into themselves as individuals.

Not only do we find it hard to let go of our kids, but we find it hard to let go of other things, like relationships or friends. Letting go of a relationship can be a horrible experience because we usually don't let go until we're totally feed up with the other person's nonsense. We stay and endure so much that sometimes we develop hatred toward the other person and that's not good! Hating someone is the last thing we want to do. That's why it's important that we let go before this happens.

Since my mom stayed and endured so much from my dad, I believe she developed hatred for him. This hatred would soon go away but because of the damage that was done, it would take years to disappear. If she had let go early in the relationship, then maybe these feelings would not have grown. There were times I would sit and watch my mother turn her head while my father did his dirt. It was hell watching my mother endure such pain as she tried desperately to let go.

Every move she made was based upon his decisions. She never drove because she depended solely on him, never even trying to get a driver's license. It was very upsetting because she even separated herself from her own mother and other family members. Her mom would pass away and never be able to see her daughter get to the point where she was dependent on herself.

Once my mother let go, she was able to look back and understand where she should have let go earlier. It is like a weight lifted off our shoulders when we finally let go. Now we don't have to pretend that we are something we're not. I say this because when we refuse to let go, we tend to do things that are pleasing to the other person and not ourselves.

I found myself deep in a situation like this for years with my son's mother. We were happy in the beginning, but that would fade away quickly. She would lose interest in me and I would find myself in the position of holding on to someone who didn't want to hold on to me, nor would I be able to let go because I had given so much of myself that I didn't know who I was anymore.

This was a bad situation because so many people told me I should leave but I just refused to listen. Things got so bad that I started denying everyone and everything just to be around this woman. It was going to take something drastic before I would let go of this situation.

Every situation is unique, though. It might not take as much for you to let go. This all depends on how deep you are involved in the situation. During our letting go process, we are not in a position to learn. It is not until we have let go and are going through our separation that we learn to elevate.

When we lost our house and my son's mother left, it was hard for me. This was the beginning of my letting go process. But it wasn't until she took my son and wouldn't let me see him then told him I never wanted to see him again that I realized that I truly had to let go. It was not only for me, but it was the best thing for my son. The decisions I made this time would alter both me and son's lives forever. When I decided that I was going to let go and went back to get my son, not only did I let go but she let go of both of us also.

When we decide to let go, we must be ready to deal with the consequences of our actions. The situation may not go as easy as we plan. We may have to deal with circumstances that we didn't expect. The good part about this is now we're in a position to make good decisions for ourselves. We are no longer making decisions based on pleasing someone else who doesn't want to be pleased.

I would be able to make good, sound decisions for me and my son. I was going through a separation and taking responsibility for what part I played in things. It was also a time when I would come to forgive myself and others who I felt played a part in my pain.

See, letting go does not mean just leaving physically, but letting go of everything inside you also: all of the hate, pain, envy, jealousy or anything that keeps you from elevating. So many times, we see this in relationships. Two people separate and because they have not let go of inner emotions, this affects the relationship with the child. Mom is so upset with dad that she talks down about the father in front of the child or she refuses to let the dad see the child and the child has to continually hear them argue.

It can also be the other way around: the father has not let go of inner emotions and refuses to see the child. In some situations, he will refuse to help the mother support the child financially. This happened several times with my dad. He refused to help my mother take care of us financially because we were not with him. And for a long time, my mom beat my dad down to us because she had not let go of her inner emotions. Whatever way it is happening, I tell you it's not right!

The purpose of us letting go is to make the situation better, not harbor our feelings. You will know when you have truly let go and released everything inside you. It's not that you have forgotten, but you have gotten past it. This will happen when you are able to sit down and have a conversation with that person you separated from negatively and not lose your cool. If you are taken out of your element every time you encounter that particular situation, then you have not let go.

One of the biggest things I have recently experience letting go was the death of my friend, Pastor Schinova Elston. This process would be extremely hard because he was a valuable part of my life. I would have to adapt to him not being around or answering my phone calls every morning. It would take a while for me to let go and not be depressed every time I heard his name or a certain song.

Eventually, I will get to the point where I will understand that he is gone but not forgotten. This is how I'm dealing with my process of letting go. I let go of the depression that keeps me from elevating and hold on the memories that bring me joy. Not only do these memories bring me joy, but they help him to live on in my mind.

If we all can learn how to let go and when to let go, we will be able to elevate in most situations. There are two parts of letting go that I think are very important. One is accepting and the other is reacting. Once you have accepted the fact that you must let go, then you must react!

You don't have to react in a negative way, but react in taking steps to prepare yourself to leave. It may not be sudden, but remember you have accepted the fact that you must let go; so start reacting and putting together a plan to leave and elevate.

The actual elevation will not take place until you have totally let go, but rest assured it will happen. Once you have let go, there is nothing else for you to do but elevate. Elevate into greatness!

FOOD FOR THOUGHT

To truly let go of something, it must not let go of you, you must let go of it!

Name something that was difficult for you to let go of before you could start your elevation:

1) _____

_____

_____

_____

_____

_____

2) _____

_____

_____

_____

_____

3) _____

_____

_____

_____

_____

SEPARATION for Elevation

4) _____
_____
_____
_____
_____
_____

5) _____
_____
_____
_____
_____
_____

TEN

I CAN SEE CLEARLY
NOW

When we reach this point in our lives, nothing can stop us from achieving our goals. You are at the point where you have accepted your separation and elevated from it. No more blaming anyone for your past failures. You have accepted whatever part you have played. There is no more battling to let go because you have let go both physically and mentally.

Even your health is better because you're not up all night trying to figure out why you're attached to something that does not want to be attached to you. Not only that, but you are ready to help others. Now you can take everything you have learned and put it to good uses by helping someone else.

I think the biggest or most important lesson that you would have learned from all this is that everything you have gone through was not about you! It was so you could be an influence to someone else. Seeing clearly is a great help to you being on the right path and staying on it.

SEPARATION for Elevation

If you've ever driven through a snowstorm or whatever, it may have been difficult to see where you were going. Sometimes, it could make you take a wrong turn and get on the wrong path. This can happen to us in life. Our vision gets so clouded with other stuff that we get totally off course. We stray from our destiny and start following a different path, usually a path that is taking us nowhere.

Sometimes you ride on this path for so long that it is hard to get back on the right one, kind of like when we're on the road driving and we miss our exit, then we get off at the next one quickly. We seek directions from various places to find out what wrong turn we took or sometimes we know the wrong turn we took. Now we get back on and we're headed back in the right direction, but it seems like it has taken hours to get back to where we started off.

You keep riding until you see something familiar. That's when you feel a sense of joy come over you. You're back on track. Now you know where you're going. Finding our way back was the hard part but now you're here and there's nothing any one can do it about it.

Once you find your way out of a storm, the entire world looks different because you have seen it through a blurry vision for so long. Now you can see everything exactly for what it is. If it's blue, it's blue! You won't mistake it for being green.

Somewhere in my father's life, I don't think he ever truly came out of his storm. I believe his vision is still blurry and he does not see past the storm. When he lost his wife and family is when his storm began, but he never evaluated from his storm. It never stopped raining in his life. Not once has he forgiven himself or others for his failures in life. His bitterness to accept the separation keeps him from elevating. This has affected his health, relationships with others and his life in general. I can see him being a great man if he would allow the storm to come to an end.

The only way he can do this is to separate, accept and elevate. When I see my mom and my siblings, I truly rejoice because we can all see clearly now. The storms we've been through have passed over now. My mom is living her life and enjoying every minute of it. My older brother is happily married and headed toward greatness in the ministry for God. Today my younger brother is being a great father to his kids and learning to live on his on.

Going through and coming out has taught me so much. The separation I've experienced has made me understand what I must do to stay focused and on course. I embrace those times that I was off course, though, because I would not be able to write this book if I didn't. I accept it all! The good and the bad. The happy and the sad.

It was all meant for me so I could help someone with this book, not only with the book, but my DVD entitled, "The Choice is Yours." A story telling the struggles one family goes through to stay together. It is an inspiration for the entire family, especially husbands and wives. This couple not only battle their differences, but they struggle to separate from disappointment in their past.

If we all get to the point where we can see clearly, then our lives become a domino effect. We walk in our destiny and it filters down to someone else and so on. If our eyes are open, then our hearts are open — open to love without boundaries. Assisting others with their needs. Helping them to achieve their goals and be the best they can be.

Everything else is laid to the side for the goodness of mankind. The bottom line to all of this is, "WE LIVE TO GIVE."

FOOD FOR THOUGHT

In order for you to lead the way, you must first be able to see the way clearly!

* All of the Food for Thoughts were written by Keith "K-Cam" Campbell.*

What things have you overcome that helped you to see your path clearly now?

1) _____

_____

_____

_____

_____

_____

2) _____

_____

_____

_____

_____

_____

3)

_____

_____

_____

_____

_____

_____

4)

_____

_____

_____

_____

_____

_____

5)

_____

_____

_____

_____

_____

_____

POSTSCRIPT

Congratulations on completing this book. I hope you took advantage of the worksheets at the end of each chapter. Now you are well on your way to understanding how to elevate from a separation in your life. I encourage you to allow your experience to be a teaching tool for someone else that may be experiencing a similar situation.

The journey is not over yet. You have just begun. Now that you have learned to elevate from your separation, you must read my next book entitled, *"Surviving Chaos, A New Beginning."* Throughout my first book, I showed how people's entire thinking changed after they elevated from their separation. It was no longer about them, but being better for the sake of mankind. Get the book because it will help you apply your knowledge from the first book to the entire world.

Be blessed!

BIOGRAPHY

Creative, artistic, and ambitious are just a few words that describe this Chicago native. Raised in Chicago, IL, **KEITH CAMPBELL** has conquered a lot of challenges that life has presented to him. Being raised in a family with two brothers and one sister, his parents have always instilled family values in their children. During a difficult time in Keith's life when his parents parted their ways this inspired Keith to start writing and acting. His love and passion for the arts has led him to write this book that helps people elevate during a separation. One of many inspirational pieces, Mr. Campbell also wrote a short film entitled *The Choice Is Yours*. A story that deals with family struggles and how we can make a choice to stick together no matter what! This young man is truly on the road to success and with a mindset to help rebuild the American family.

www.ingramcontent.com/pod-product-compliance
Lightning Source LLC
Chambersburg PA
CBHW060955040426
42445CB00011B/1167